Metamorphosis

Metamorphosis

POEMS *from*
the **WILDERNESS**

Jordyn Wyldflower

Unless otherwise noted, Scripture quotations and paraphrased material are from the King James Version (KJV), which is in the public domain.

Scripture quotations and paraphrased material marked (NIV) are taken from the Holy Bible, New International Version®, NIV®. Copyright © 1973, 1978, 1984, 2011 by Biblica, Inc.® Used by permission. All rights reserved worldwide.

First edition, 2025
ISBN: 979-8-9999406-0-5

Book cover and interior design by the brilliant Boštjan Lisec

Therefore, if anyone is in Christ,
the new creation has come:
The old has gone, the new is here!

-2 Corinthians 5:17 (NIV)

....

Whoever finds their life will lose it,
and whoever loses their life
for my sake will find it.

-Matthew 10:39 (NIV)

....

And we all, who with unveiled faces
contemplate the Lord's glory, are
being transformed into his image with
ever-increasing glory, which comes
from the Lord, who is the Spirit.

-2 Corinthians 3:18 (NIV)

Dedication

This book of poems is dedicated to honoring my nephew Nathan who was my favorite person and the divine messenger and catalyst for my metamorphosis. Yours was an excruciatingly difficult yet powerful and impactful mission. You were the true embodiment of unconditional love, courage, superhuman strength, truth, wisdom, gratitude, joy, creativity, acceptance and hope. Your life and love helped me find my wings. Hope you are enjoying yours in heaven sweet angel.

Contents

Acknowledgements

This book would not have been possible without the goodness of God and the assistance of my guides. I invited them into my writing process often and asked them to help me express what wanted to be expressed through me. Special thanks to my dear friend Dianna for her loving encouragement and for sharing her sunflower and tiger energies with me. Big thank you to my dad for his unwavering support and for being a source of light throughout my life. Thank you to the spiritual mentors I've learned from over the years, the creativity experts who have opened my eyes to a new way of experiencing the world, and the poets, musicians, and content creators who inspired me with their messages and helped me gain the courage to share my own.

Introduction

// "The greatest miracle is the inner metamorphosis of a human being" –Amma. I bought a magnet with this quote on it long before the start of my metamorphosis. My soul must have known what was coming. Truth be told, if I had known what this process entailed ahead of time I can't say whether I would have chosen it. It has been a painful, lonely, confusing, and sometimes terrifying roller coaster of emotions. Some moments I felt like I was in total euphoria bubbling over with joy, and other moments I felt like my life had no purpose and I didn't want to live, sometimes within the same day. That being said, it has been the most rewarding and fruitful experience of my life, and I am proud of myself for continuing to show up, and extremely grateful for how this journey has changed me in ways so profound that I am still discovering them. The journey is less about where you're going or what you are achieving and more about who you are becoming. This book was my first time expressing my heart through this art form of poetry and I have enjoyed it immensely. I started writing to process and understand what I was going through, and finished writing with the hope that my words could help others undergoing a similar transformation. I pray my words will provide you with support, hope and some light through the darker moments. If you are going through it I want you to know that I see you and you are not alone and you are so much stronger than you think (and you are not doing it wrong ☺). Changing your life starts with going within. It will be so worth it and you are worthy of your own love and attention. We have work to do in this moment of mass evolution of human consciousness on earth. The path of faith doesn't promise a life without difficulties but rather equips and strengthens us for them. And we can rely on God always and in all ways. This process might be tough but we are tougher. I'm rooting for you!

Metamorphosis

Behold this sacred journey led by faith in the Divine
a restoration of beings to original design
a journey of becoming, reborn and made new
awakening and seeing beyond the veil to what is true
an absolute transformation in nature and form
initiated by a dark period of the soul
there is no map to follow, no pre-known destination
the GPS is your own heart and intuitive communication
the wilderness, the space where you're neither here nor there
requiring trust and patience as you're gradually made aware
the focus is internal, set apart to go within
integrating shadows and healing all that's been
blinding us from seeing the truth of who we are
powerful, unlimited love made from the stars
no longer in survival and lack we can perceive
the abundance of provision and possibilities
transcending the illusions of fear and separation
conscious God is in us and we are one with all creation
the process can be taxing with intense highs and lows
but his grace is sufficient[1] to hold us through our woes
surrendering and aligning further each step of the way
expanding with higher peace and grateful presence every day
letting go of the false self, embracing new beginnings
emerging more authentic and resilient beings
a lighter version filled with hope, purpose and resolve
how beautiful is this journey of answering the Divine call

Black Sheep

A rose gave birth to a wildflower
that wildflower was me
no matter how hard I tried
a rose I couldn't be
I made myself into a pretzel
made choices just for her
lost weight, dressed nice
smiled and nodded
in a small pot of toxic soil
the little girl inside me
became a chameleon
she tip toed around the others
afraid to rock the boat
but decades of tip toeing
came with a steep price
one day she looked in the mirror
and had no idea who she was
the molding had led her down a path
that wasn't meant for her
and suddenly she found herself
lost in the wilderness
confused, alone and scared
she turned up towards the sun
basking in the love she had always longed for
realizing she had been a wildflower all along
she wasn't meant to be confined or be like the other flowers
she was meant to create a path led by her own heart
it took some time to root herself into gentler soil
where she could finally be herself and finally feel whole

Purging Darkness

My heart, what are you feeling?
nausea from all the releasing
trauma like an open wound
dredging through the mud of triggers
hypervigilant, startled, looking over my shoulder
big dark shadows, I cower and shiver
stains covering the once white walls
spiders lurking around every corner
constricted and trapped, mind is small
nervous, alone, vulnerable in the dark
then I remember my heart has a light
I look up at the heavens, the moon, the stars
I'm not alone at all, just needed to see
this darkness that has been plaguing me
feel it to heal it, isn't that what they say?
reminding myself that I am ok
I am not this trauma, this fear, this unrest
or the stories I told myself about what it meant
it's time to let go, to move on, to start fresh
to make room for the magic that patiently awaits
the birds singing outside seem to agree
it's time to fly dear one, it's time to be free

Inner Work

I once had a job, a nine to five
I gave all of myself in an effort to thrive
exhausted and drained after every day
I knew there had to be another way
I was passionate about helping people be their best selves
yet I didn't extend this same care to myself
a wounded healer giving all my love out
while my starved inner child had to make do without
compassion fatigue signaled it was too much
the security of the paycheck just wasn't enough
drowning in a sea of grief and pain
my usual coping could no longer sustain
after a decade of giving my blood sweat and tears
I was giving my notice while grappling with fears
the time was nigh for my focus to shift
to answer the call to journey within
to connect with my heart, my spirit, my soul
accepting all parts of me, becoming more whole
releasing old programs and patterns and beliefs
understanding my worth and finding my peace
discovering my purpose and who I truly am
surrendering and trusting in God's divine plan
reclaiming my power and freedom of choice
embracing creativity and finding my voice
these fruits of my labor didn't blossom overnight
at times it felt like I was fighting for my life
facing your demons takes courage and strength
only made possible with that mustard seed of faith
with the light of my awareness and unconditional love

I'm becoming the person I have always dreamed of
while the inner work won't directly pay the bills
the rewards are exponential and promise to fulfill
as this mystical path leads to wondrous new places
my cup runneth over[2] with amazing graces

Full Moon Release

Everything comes up to the surface
crimson tides of disappointment
let it go let it go let it go
tears of rage, I see red
aching in my lower belly
dance it out, sing it out, cry it out, howl it out
numbing distracting avoiding escaping
purging toxicity from all my pores
fetal position under the moonlight
somehow I have let everyone down
somehow I am finally not letting myself down
the guilt, the shame, the judgment, the obligation
can't go on living in that kind of oppression
if you don't come to me with loving intention
I am no longer home, don't leave a message

Mother Wound

let mother hear your cries
let mother wipe your tears
let mother see your pain
let her mirror the same
let mother know your fears
let mother hold you dear
let mother witness the messy parts
let mother soothe your aching heart
let mother know your deepest needs
let her nurture you with caring deeds
let mother in to feel it all
let mother answer your tender call

when did I realize she couldn't feed me?
when did I decide I wouldn't need her?
when did she feel this about her own mother?
how many daughters before me have cried themselves to sleep,
        anguished and afraid?
when will we let love heal this pervasive pain?
Mother Mary help me break this generational chain
no more unloved daughters becoming wounded mothers

Hatred Is a Poison

Hatred is a poison running through my veins
there is no part of me that is left untouched
it slowly steals my empathy, my clarity, my peace
feeding me lies about the past while devouring my now
it tells me I'm a victim and that justice must be served
collecting its army of bitterness, resentment and rage
it drains the colors from my vision and fills me with disdain
sneaky, insatiable, slithering through undetected
wreaking havoc on my system and all to which I am connected
it is prideful and self-righteous and it makes me want to scream
providing faulty data so I won't doubt its validity
what am I to do when I detect this poison in my being?
God give me the antidote to flush these toxins out my cells
it starts with love and forgiveness, especially for myself
accepting the invitation to delve into the wounded self
aware that carrying venom only puts me in harm's way
appreciating the growth that's been initiated by this pain
remembering whose I am and what I came here for
to learn, to heal, to know my worth
trusting that justice is not mine to exact
telling the little girl inside me I've got her back
since we are all one and in this together
we can't be running around poisoning one another
let us each be responsible for our own systems
noticing when we've been hijacked and fooled by the trickster
reminding ourselves who we are and what we can achieve
when we let the light shine where the hatred used to be

Cleaning

Lately I've noticed that when I clean
things are dirtier than they initially seemed
dust I didn't even realize was there
camouflaged lint, unseen strands of hair
in order for something to really be cleaned
the dirt and the grime must be exposed and seen
cloths become filthier, towels made wetter
it seems to get worse before it gets better
it's something akin to the process of healing
one moment I'm fine, then life triggers a feeling
suddenly the gunk I didn't know was there
rises to the surface to make me aware
when I try to ignore it or push it away
it comes back even louder determined to stay
until it's acknowledged and further explored
remind myself even dirty I'm worthy and adored
attending to the wound that has been reopened
the judgment, the shame, releasing emotions
old beliefs and patterns that no longer fit
victim mentality transmuting to grit
cleaning ain't easy but it's always worth it

Letting Go

Every time I say goodbye a piece of me disappears
loved ones who have passed on
past lovers who were not the one
old friends who begin to drift
harmful dynamics that no longer fit
many times I have held on too long
attached to people who were all wrong
seeking water in dry wells
giving all of me in return for crumbs
after so much heartbreak and pain
some valuable insights I have gained
there are seasons in our lives
through which people come and go
some are here for the long haul
and some are just a cameo
everyone's a mirror
revealing aspects of ourselves
projecting parts of themselves
role-playing our own realities
nothing is personal
and yet everything is
identity is ego that I long to transcend
we are all each other's teachers
and students as well
no one belongs on a pedestal
or warrants devaluing either
in the ways that matter we are all equal
everyone I've crossed paths with has played a crucial role
whether loving or uncaring I'm grateful to them all

for leading me back to the most valuable relationship there will ever be
in truth it was always about my relationship with me
and of course the loving God who created and sustains me
and while goodbyes still fill me with deep sorrow and grief
and sometimes I still grapple with abandonment fears
I realize now with every goodbye a piece of me appears

Ocean Message

Last night I dreamt about a high ocean tide
big scary waves toppling everything in sight
washing away belongings as they retreat from the shore
foretelling of shifts and changes galore
feeling overwhelmed with nowhere to hide
I have no control or support by my side
something is happening, I wish I knew what
the wind is a herald of a future undefined
as I smell the salty air I remember to breathe
rooting into the sand as if I were a tree
I gaze up at the sun, let it bathe me in light
and suddenly I realize everything is alright
more than alright, it's actually great
the waves have reached a more tranquil state
mirroring my serenity they ripple and sway
twinkling under the sunlight, it's a beautiful day!
In this new state I'm receptive to hearing
the ocean's message of wisdom and healing:

The past is being cleansed now so you can rebuild
a new life where your wildest dreams are fulfilled
the sea gives and the sea clears away[3]
letting go with grace is the optimal way
venturing into waters shallow and profound
remember your life guard is always around
it is not recommended to look too far ahead
the size of the waves may cause needless dread

stay present and notice that once they arrive
they're smaller and gentler than you visualized
trust in your ability to swim through these shifts
flow with the current and appreciate the gifts

Sisters

Your sister is your God-given first best friend
she holds you when you're born and hands you down her things
showing you how to walk and talk and play and read and share
you worship her like an idol and hope she'll always be there
but what if the sister God gave you wishes you were never born?
what if she sees your presence as a distraction and a threat?
what if she thinks you're annoying and embarrassing in front
    of her friends?
what if she sees you as competition for the approval she so craves?
maybe I'm just projecting, maybe it's all my stuff
maybe my mother never really taught her how to love
maybe the reason she judges me is because she hates herself
maybe she can't stand to witness my freedom from her prison cell
maybe she wishes I could be a little more like her
following a well-worn path and abiding by all the rules
living by the checklist that we were handed down
appearances over substance, inauthenticity abounds
somehow I can't reach her, can't see who she really is
maybe her walls are up so high because of her own pain
she's never understood me, never really tried
keeping me at arms length, yet wanting me by her side?
nothing would make me happier than to feel my sister's love
if only I believed it was something she was capable of
I never lose hope that one day things could change
that my big sister could hold me in a warm embrace
ice thawed between us, our inner children could play
after all, your sister is your God-given first best friend

Safe Space

My father was my first human taste of God
always present, ever-loving, he was my rock
provider, protector, gently buffering me
from the harsh realities I was yet to see
with him I always knew where I stood
from his excitement upon seeing me, I understood
in his presence he wanted me to feel at home
when I called, he invariably picked up the phone
he supported me financially long after required
with no strings attached, his generosity inspired
though he came from a culture that prioritized men
he never made me feel like I was any less than
he still insists on holding the door open for me
and at the same time he respects my agency
lighthearted and playful, forever young at heart
he taught me to read with the words poo, pee and fart
carrying so much responsibility on his shoulders
never letting on about the weight of those boulders
instead he told dad jokes and gave humorous nicknames
taking challenges in stride and playing life as a game
with the memory of an elephant and the intelligence of a savant
charismatic and humble, with values any daughter would want
of course he's not perfect, always putting others first
this can sometimes work as a blessing and a curse
he sees the best in people and reflects it back to them
accepting me for who I am even when he doesn't quite comprehend
I couldn't be more grateful for his unconditional love
my harmony loving papa, the personification of a dove
although God couldn't be my earthly human father
he chose the most amazing surrogate for me, his daughter

Going Places Alone

I used to be the person surrounded by friends
collecting them like there was a prize at the end
somehow I felt that if everyone liked me
the critical voice in my head would be silenced
big birthday bashes were evidence of my value
social anxiety quelled by imbibing with company
going somewhere alone felt akin to self-torcher
insecurities made me want to hide in a corner
but lately something inside me has changed
and solitude is something I suddenly crave
my focus has gone from outside to within
to following the whisper of my intuition
my heart is my compass, my ego in retreat
getting out of my comfort zone was a great feat
with wonder I head out to see what life brings
letting my guides plan it all out for me
what will I experience? who will I meet?
maybe I'll walk around barefoot or connect with a tree
there's magic to behold when I live in the flow
when I let life surprise me somehow it knows
the secret I've learned from going places on my own
is that it's actually a fallacy, we're never truly alone

Rumination

When I find myself having faux conversations in my head
trying to rewrite history or prove a point to manage dread
playing it over and over and dwelling on a loop
noticing the impact this is having on my mood
one day I interrupted with intention to bring in light
I turned the whole thing over to the one who can make it right
shifting into prayer transformed helplessness to hope
talking it out with God was a healthier way to cope
letting my inner child know no matter how she feels
that her concerns are valid and her pain is real
changing my perspective to the view from up above
receiving reassurance that I am safe and loved
next time I am ruminating and spinning in my mind
I will free myself by focusing on the Divine

Eden

The snake was wrong. Still is.
we must not fear it
we must not run away from it
we must gently tame it
it can only hurt us if we agree with it[4]

Under the Covers

Last night I dreamt of tossing out blankets
layers of protection I once held onto
hiding my true self beneath a duvet
melting into the comfort of a fuzzy embrace
nobody else was welcome there
in my self-made refuge for escaping the fear
after a while it felt lonely and dark
so I lifted a corner to let in some light
in my illumined nest I could be a work in progress
judgment and expectations slowly fell away
I have learned to love the sweet girl hiding in the blanket
and she knows now she's safe to be just as she is
so maybe she's ready to come out of hiding
to throw off the armor and tiptoe on out
or better yet skip and dance her way out
delighting herself in this spacious new freedom
she knows her shine is quite needed in the world
she can't go on hiding it under the covers
no longer cloaked in shame, feeling worthless and small
draped in his robe of righteousness[5] she can conquer it all
a cherished child of God with a calling on her life
she is learning to walk in grace with her head held high

Giving Away My Power

Let me count the ways I have given away my power:

I have been a chameleon changing colors depending on my
surroundings
I have made myself small and quiet in public spaces
I have said sorry when I had nothing to be sorry for
I have seen my presence as an inconvenience or burden for others
I have smiled and nodded when I didn't feel right about something
I have said maybe when I meant no
I have said yes when I meant no
I have stayed quiet when I wanted to scream
I have failed to set boundaries and have allowed people to violate
them
I have put on masks and changed my behavior to make myself
palatable to others
I have believed that I only deserve love when I act or look a certain
way
I have yo-yo dieted out of a desire to "fix" my body so that someone
will love me
I have said I don't care what we do or where we go even when I did
care
I have insisted someone take the last bite of a shared dish when I
wanted it
I have compared myself to other people and deemed them
better than me
I have listened to what others said about how I should live my life
I have made decisions to please my parents over myself in an attempt
to gain approval

I have walked the path someone else laid out for me as a trap
I have ruminated about why I didn't hear back from someone
and what I did wrong
I have been emotionally reactive and acted impulsively
I have believed that my worth is up for debate
I have measured myself through my appearance, my
accomplishments, my intelligence, my education, my age, my
possessions, my marital and parental status, the list goes on
I have sought validation from everyone but myself
I have allowed my body to be objectified and used
I have allowed others to define me based on their projections
I have blamed myself for things that weren't my fault
I have complained, seen myself as a victim and felt sorry for myself
I have hidden away parts of myself out of fear of rejection or
abandonment
I have given comparison, judgment, obligation, guilt and shame a seat
at my table
I have overruled my intuition and made decisions based in fear, ego
and programming
I have let cultural and social expectations override my values
and authenticity
I have put people with questionable intentions on a pedestal and
followed them
I have partaken in chisme to gain favor and fit in
I have put others' needs first and left my inner child to fend for herself
I have walked on egg shells around people in the name of "keeping
the peace"
I have enabled others and made excuses for inexcusable behavior

I have trusted people who didn't deserve my trust
I have let the fear of failure stop me from trying
I have used food, travel, socializing, shopping etc. as a means
      of escape and validation
I have dressed for the male gaze
I have dressed for the female gaze
I have dressed for the wealthy gaze
I have dressed for the humble gaze
I have dressed in ways to blend in
I have dressed in ways to stand out
I have dressed in ways to blend in while standing out

I am exhausted. I am DONE.

New Shoes

I ordered a pair of black Toms sandals from the internet
and when the box arrived those shoes were nowhere to be found
instead what I received was a cream sandal of a different style
a pair of shoes I never would have ordered for myself
I tried them on anyway out of curiosity
and what I found were sandals that were perfect just for me
they might be the most comfortable shoes I've ever put on
matching every outfit, elevating my fashion
although I never would have given these shoes a second look
I realize when ordering the faulty path I took
trying to buy a pair of shoes that looked like ones I've worn
tried and true, familiar, staying in my comfort zone
a knowing smile aware that these things happen for a reason
acknowledging that in my life I've entered a new season
the shoes that got me here to the place I am today
are not the same as the ones I need to continue on my way
when Jesus takes the wheel he also takes the shopping cart
knowing my every need, his thoughtful love is a work of art
sending me opportunities that I alone would miss
being a child of God means even mistakes can lead to bliss[6]

Inner Child

Standing at a corner waiting to cross the street
a little girl aged 4 or 5 mumbled something to me
I thought about ignoring her and acting like I didn't hear
instead I asked her to repeat herself and drew myself near
she expressed excitement that we were crossing at the same time
and that we were both with men, her with her dad, me with mine
endeared by her desire to connect I put on a playful tone
and asked about what she was holding, a little unicorn
I told her that I wished I had a unicorn as well
or better yet with my imagination I could become one myself
in that moment I saw the little girl's eyes light up
a new world of possibility seemed to open up
she realized she too could become a unicorn like me
and together we spontaneously galloped across the street
I was no longer a middle aged woman, proper and poised
I was a girl having fun playing pretend and cheerfully making noise
forgetting about how I looked or what other people thought
suspending all judgment and shoulds and should nots
I allowed my inner child to come out and play
never minding that grown ups rarely act this way
when we reached the other side of the street and had to part ways
the smiling girl blew me a kiss goodbye and I did the same
our short-lived encounter was the highlight of my day
I was grateful to this sweet girl for engaging with me this way
an oft overlooked part of me felt quite seen and free
touching my heart and soul so very deeply
I hope our brief exchange made an impact on her too
as a child I myself could've used an imaginative adult or two
perhaps then rather than having caused me distress

my genuine self would have felt safer being expressed
I've come to understand that this little girl was me
an external projection of my essence unseen
reflecting who I had been all those years ago
before I was conditioned to put on a mask and a show
reconnecting with my inner child, what a precious gift
sometimes all you have to do is cross the street to come
        home to yourself

Grief

How strange it feels when your whole world comes crashing down
and yet it's business as usual when you look around
don't they see that nothing will ever be the same?
emotions are too intense and confusing to name
shock and denial, could this reality be real?
bargaining with circumstances, desperate for a deal
anger and sadness as the mind seeks to find blame
what could I have done to prevent this dreadful change?
despair over an imagined future that will never be
tears are a necessary avenue for release
stomach is in knots as anxiety hits
fielding worse case scenarios as the future looks grim
heartbroken and vulnerable I seek comfort and hope
faith is my lifeline and humor helps me cope
being gentle with myself and allowing what is
listening to my body, providing what it needs
movement, nature, music, water, food and rest
support from loved ones who love me best
looking for silver linings and making meaning of the loss
the rainbow, the lotus, the light through the cracks
staying connected to my heart as I learn to let go
I find greater acceptance knowing God is in control
gratitude is key to making it through
for the love, for the memories, and for how much I grew
thank you grief for teaching me the preciousness of life
and to relish every moment with presence and delight

Bible

The bible is a portal to another realm
a place where I can meet the one always at the helm
where I can get to know him, his character, his ways
and be lovingly guided through confusion on hard days

The bible is a living breathing document to me
with the author often clarifying precisely what he means
informing how to apply his teachings to my specific life
edifying with wisdom for overcoming worldly strife

The bible is a testament of human evolution
it's not a set of directions but rather provides a blueprint
for spiritual transformation as we become more like him
signaling where we're headed, where we are and where we've been

The bible is a light source illuminating the path for me
from darkness I've been plagued with to a soul set free
with parables and layers it meets us where we are
anchoring us in the present while inspiring us to go far

The bible is a weapon for use in spiritual ordeals
as he prepares us for our calling he gradually reveals
it hasn't always been used with noble intention
but the truth always prevails with divine intervention

The bible is a mirror reflecting my faith's maturity
whether or not it's literal it is vastly enlightening
comforted and healed by sacred parallels I see
the bible leads me back home to the Spirit in me

More Light

As more light comes in
as the healing occurs
that which is out of resonance
comes up to be purged

As more light comes in
as the healing goes on
the seeds are being planted
for who I am to become

As more light comes in
as the healing gets deeper
it is almost as if
I am two different people

As more light comes in
and true healing is here
emotions are oscillating
between love and fear

As more light comes in
as the healing proceeds
the intensity is dialed up
on these contrasting energies

As more light comes in
and earth mother is healing
the shadows of yesterday
are in violent revealing

As more light comes in
and we heal universally
we must keep our focus
on the world we prefer to see

As more light comes in
and the healing is divine
let us fortify one another
as we allow ourselves to shine

Dear Inner Child

My sweet honey, you are so precious, valuable, brilliant, magical, radiant, beautiful inside and out. I love you unconditionally and accept you exactly as you are because you are perfectly imperfect and uniquely you. You are a blessing to this world and your gifts are exactly what this world needs. Let your light shine bright my darling girl! I am here for you always to support you, your feelings are valid and you are safe with me. You have no need to worry, you can relax, you can exhale, you can play and laugh and feel joy. Everything is going to be more than ok. You can let go of control, you don't have to please anyone or perform, you can just be you and allow yourself to be taken care of. I've got you, God's got you, your guides and angels have got you, you are surrounded by warmth and love always.

My Body

my body is perfect, created in his image
my body changes and that's okay
my worth is not based on my body
my body is home and I take great care of it
my body is a precious gift from God and a sacred temple in
      which his Spirit dwells[7]
I am sorry body for the times I have hurt you and allowed others
      to hurt you, please forgive me
thank you body for all the amazing things you do and all
      the ways you allow me to experience and enjoy life
my body is healthy, strong and resilient
my body is intelligent and knows how to heal
my body is an invaluable source of wisdom and information
      for my life's journey
my body is worthy of my love always; I love and accept you body
my body is made new in this sacred rebirth process
my body is light and ready for flight

Mirror

Looking out at all I see
everything points back to me
nothing's ever just out there
triggers making me aware
of reactions that reveal
aspects of me yet to heal
maybe I have buried them
maybe from lives past
maybe they're too hard to own
projected or out-cast
witnessing the emotions
letting them move through
examining patterns and beliefs
releasing for something new
life then is a mirror
reflecting back to me
all my inner world
so I can mend and be set free
isn't that so terrifying
taking responsibility
isn't it empowering
knowing the answers lie in me
focusing within thus becomes a potent way
to change our outer circumstances and even shift our day
blaming and complaining only rob me of this truth
self-fulfilling prophecies can serve us faulty proof

perceiving our experiences as happening *to* us
enlightened now to know they're happening *from* and *for* us
awakening to the reality of what we're here to do
evolving to higher consciousness, learning in earth school
looking out at all I see
everything is serving me

Keep Your Eyes on Me

Keep your eyes on me my child
pay no heed to the happenings of the day
the news on TV, the strife, the unrest
there is much competition for your valuable gaze
as the past incessantly knocks on your door
and the enemy attempts to slither into your mind
the world anxious to convince you of all the things you need to buy
to keep up with the Joneses and your faux worth high
your energy is a precious resource you must allocate wisely
I am doing a new thing in you[8] that requires discernment
I need you in the moment in your body in the flow
connected to your heart facing whatever the mirrors show
eating nourishing foods and getting plenty of rest
the answers aren't outside of you, your inner compass knows best
I need you to trust my timing, and let go of control
have patience through the process and meet your struggles with love
let nature be your charger, hug that tree, feet on the earth
embody nonresistance, find gratitude even when it hurts
this path is not an easy one child, not everyone will choose it
it might feel like you're different and have trouble finding your place
I didn't create you to fit in to this world but rather to blaze a trail
to light the way for others with my loving presence through yours
I am always by your side, holding your hand each step of the way
made perfect in your weakness[9] so lean on me on harder days
I am your strength, song and salvation[10], turn your burdens over to me[11]
seeing things from my perspective will help you navigate with
    more ease

we're in this together child, we have work to do
I can't wait to reveal all the blessings I have for you
but you can't get distracted by the chaos and the noise
keep your eyes on me my child, and the keys will soon be yours[12]

Built on a Rock

In the midst of the storm holding on for dear life
a spiritual initiation packed with internal strife
doing drills in the water, gasping for air
my mind is a battleground for spiritual warfare
being tested and equipped for what is to come
remaining vigilant of where the orders are coming from
a struggling dove that has been caught in a net
a pulsing sensation on the side of my head
the net seems to be made of my own thoughts and beliefs
an amalgamation of old wounds, trauma and grief
as I try and bathe some of the darkness off
a knowingness enters, a light bulb turns on
you are under attack because of how valuable you are
and no weapon formed against you[13] will get very far
you can breathe under water, your will is that strong
take refuge in his arms[14] and keep on keeping on
with patience, persistence and unwavering love
the net will disintegrate and liberate the dove
there is nothing to fear and no way to fail
with faith built on a rock you will always prevail[15]

Death and Rebirth

Last night I dreamt I was dying of cancer
giving final directives on what to do with my body
I woke up with an aching pain in my heart
understanding now the sobbing from earlier that night
grieving the past self that is continually disappearing
releasing the parts of me that were never me at all

It reminded me of a dream I had last year
that one was much darker and shrouded in fear
under spiritual attack by those I loved
they celebrated they'd managed to hurt me so much
in that dream I was also dying
but in waking state I wasn't sure I would make it out alive

This time feels so different, since I accepted him into my heart
since he pulled me out of the depths and helped me find my inner light
"it's time for resurrection," he whispered in my ear
since he defeated death for eternal life, I know I needn't fear
the same Spirit that raised him from the grave lives inside of me
each time I'm reborn I am more the person he created me to be[16]

Between Two Selves

I have been in this bubble for several years now
suspended in time, somewhere between the old and new
a quiet solo journey to the very depths of my being
unmasking, unearthing, and unlearning too
embracing a stance of acceptance and trusting the Divine
reconnecting with my essence, allowing my light to shine
learning to love my body, my inner child, my soul
remembering who I am, integrating parts to feel whole
a foreign sense of peace has washed over me
and yet every night sleep seems to elude me
on the verge of tears at a moment's notice
standing still but buzzing with anticipation
tuning into my heart to understand what this means
an image of how I am standing somewhere in between
my left foot in the past, my right foot in the future
as they get further away my legs lower slowly into the splits
I understand now the complexity of my emotions
the grief over all that has been lost
the peace a taste of the promises from God[17]
unable to fall asleep due to fears of the unknown
the anticipation of knowing the time to jump has come
God give me the courage to take this leap of faith
to the timeline where your miracles and wonders await

Breaking Out

Lately it feels like the walls are caving in
the pressure around me continues to build
the view out the window has splendidly changed
yet inside me the chaos and confusion remain
waiting an eternity on promises made
up all night, thoughts swirling through my head
grasping for the hope and serenity I foretasted
I wonder if I made a wrong turn along the way
braving the ocean looking for answers
salt water clearing the dirt off my lenses
my unfurled wings are crumpled and wet
as I continue to build muscle in the Christalis
summoning patience when I'm feeling defeated
deeply surrendering as this conversion is completed
like a diamond formed with high heat and stress
this purification takes time and finesse
allowing for things to unfold as they must
reminding myself to continue to trust
to rest and self-nourish to have the strength
for labor is known to be riddled with pain
crowning has taken on multiple meanings[18]
as I await divine timing to emerge a sacred being

An Opening

Every day I wake up with existential dread
thoughts about the day running circles in my head
how to face the nothingness of having no plans
no job, no family, endless time on my hands
wondering about my purpose and why God has me here
isolated, fatigued, impatient and in fear
feeling stuck while beneath the surface vast changes go on
sometimes I can't help but venture into rumination
making up to-do lists in an effort to feel safe
why is it so hard to relish this wilderness space
after decades of avoiding truly facing myself
feeling daunted by discoveries and emotionally overwhelmed
giving pep talks to my inner child to help her understand
the worrier in me is no longer in command
with Jesus at the wheel and trauma in the rearview
she can finally exhale and enjoy the scenic view
an opening, as I dip my toe in the possibility
that it's safe to let go and allow in God's peace
that I can face every day with presence and delight
following my joy and soaring to new heights
what's so scary about the unknown after all
the mission must be important when the order is so tall

Presence

it is safe to be in my body
it is safe to enjoy the breeze
it is safe to gaze at the trees
it is safe to feel the sun shine on me
it is safe for my mind to be at ease
it is safe to just BE

Love You from a Distance

I know it's been hard to say goodbye
after so many years of having me by your side
I was a devoted family member and committed friend
it's hard to come to terms with never seeing you again
I realize God put you in my life for a reason
just starting to understand it was only for some seasons
after a lifetime of putting the needs of others first
I have finally learned to love myself and know my worth
as I've focused on healing and reclaimed my power
my relationships have largely become estranged and soured
it has taken some years to heal deep wounds and hidden anger
working through trauma trusting I'm no longer in danger
Father forgive them for they know not what they do[19]
Father forgive me for hurting myself and others too
I do miss you at times and grieve the future we imagined
I have worked to see my role in things and muster up compassion
I know you are hurting and never meant to cause pain
but I can no longer absorb it, I must stay in my own lane
I can no longer make myself who you need me to be
I can't stay in dynamics that are damaging for me
after putting my inner child in harm's way for ages
I will protect her at ALL costs and help her out of mental cages
I will let her be creative and let her express her voice
let her be her most authentic self and know that she has choice
in fact I had to make a choice between you and me
and though it wasn't easy, I am finally choosing me
I'm sorry for any pain I've caused and hope your heart will heal
I'll treasure our good memories, even be grateful for our ordeal
thank you for the growth inspired by our connection

I will take what I have learned as I go in a new direction
acknowledging that God works in mysterious ways
who knows if it will be his will to cross our paths some day
and though we must diverge in this moment of existence
I will pray on your behalf and wish to love you from a distance

I Trust You

My life looks nothing like I expected it would
struggling with acceptance, swimming in shoulds
many nights I've cried out to you asking you why
wondering if you've forgotten me or if I'm doing this right
did I take a wrong turn or somehow lose your favor
what if I'm not strong enough to see this thing through
maybe I have trust issues, grappling with surrender
wondering if your love is earned and if I'm worthy and deserving
forgive me for I know this is not how your love works
it's just that those entrusted with loving me have inflicted some hurt
and when I pray I must admit my faith has been wanting
I speak the words but wonder if you'll hear them and answer
I'm finally ready to exit off this misleading path of doubt
seeing now my lack of trust is what this struggle's been about
fear and undeserving blocked my ability to receive
projecting human limitation onto perfect divinity
so this is my declaration, in full sincerity:

I trust you will all my heart and all my soul and all my mind[20]
I trust that you hear my prayers and that you take them seriously
I trust that if I keep knocking you will open eventually[21]
I trust that you know me better than I even know myself
I trust that you love me always even when I'm not my best
I trust that you have a plan for me that's better than I could imagine
I trust that when I'm in tears you surround me with your compassion
I trust that you use my hardships and challenges for good[22]

I trust that you give me strength when I feel exhausted and weak[23]
I trust that you are deliberate in what you reveal to me
I trust that you are the light that illuminates my path
I trust that you're a perfect Father full of care and wisdom
I trust that your grace is boundless and your love is without conditions
I trust that you've mended my broken heart more times than I could
    count
I trust that you're my provider, protector and confidant
I trust that the fulfillment I seek can only be found in you
I trust that you are my greatest inspiration, my muse
I trust in the freedom and empowerment that your guidance provides
I trust in your peace, your joy and your promise that I can fly
I trust that you're always rooting for me and helping me to grow
I trust that you are the same yesterday, today and tomorrow[24]
I trust in your plans to prosper me and give me a future and hope[25]
I trust in the awesome news that your Son came to promote
I trust that with your Spirit in me there's nothing I cannot do
I trust that the reason I've got this is because I've got you
I trust that you want to ease my burdens and make my path straight[26]
I trust in you forever with my mustard seed of faith[27]

New Name

When I was born I was given a Hebrew name
a custom with Jewish newborns for ritual's sake
I rarely thought about it or even heard it mentioned
a dormant identity with hardly any felt connection
little did I know this name contained the seed
for a future self that was always meant to be
Yardena, signifying flowing down
after the Jordan River with history so profound
leading from the wilderness to the Promised Land[28]
a symbol of freedom for Israelites by God's mighty hand
the site where Christ was baptized with the Holy Spirit[29]
offering rebirth, sacred purity and union with Spirit
embarking on my own journey of freedom and rebirth
I felt a nudge to revisit the names given me at birth
the further I transformed my old name Janet ceased to fit
like many other aspects I had seemingly outgrown it
learning about my Hebrew name I was pleasantly surprised
I played with it in language and form until it felt just right
I knew it was time to step into my divine identity
with a name that felt aligned with this emerging version of me
how empowering it felt to select my own name
once I let go of the fears of what others would say
and just like any change it has been a work in progress
with novel revelations throughout the becoming process
as I embody Jordyn I feel more ready to reap
the abundant harvest that has always been my destiny

Proclamation-Inner Child Day

Whereas, adulting has been reduced to work, checklist items, chores, paying bills, and other responsibilities; and

Whereas, the world outside feels heavy and hate-filled and dark; and

Whereas, many of the ways we have been conditioned to think, feel and behave are entirely upside down and soul crushing; now therefore

Be it proclaimed that on the day of my inner child's choosing, I, by virtue of the authority vested in me as her adult, do hereby proclaim Inner Child Day. This day will be one of pure play, curiosity, imagination, creativity and fun. This day will be heart-led and there will be no rules. This day is established in recognition of my inner child's worthiness to enjoy her life, relax, receive and be delighted. All of her wishes will be granted; none will be denied. The train has left the station. Choo choo.

Letter to My Past Self

Dear Janet,

The time has come for me to move on
to reap the fruits of all I have sown
to unfurl these wings and learn how to fly
to enter my promised land, I must say goodbye:

goodbye to the trauma, resentment and fear
goodbye to old patterns and beliefs I held dear
goodbye to seeking answers outside of myself
goodbye to pleasing others while my needs were shelved

goodbye to the judgment, the guilt and the shame
goodbye to being the target of my criticism and blame
goodbye to addictions, avoidance, fight or flight
goodbye to unworthiness and dimming my light

living in survival mode took an enormous toll on you
I'm proud of you for how you navigated and made it through
the journey has been laden with hardship and pain
yet your gentle and beautiful heart has remained

thank you for your hope, your curiosity and your strength
thank you for your truth seeking and courage along the way
thank you for never giving up on the sense that you were meant for more
thank you for waking up to the truth of who and whose we really are

by the grace of God I have been called to a new life
trudging through the darkness, I have finally found some light
the best parts of you will always be with me
I will love you forever, unequivocally

Love always,
Jordyn

Newborn

Father, as I am reborn, I will require your assistance
show me how to adjust to this new body and frequency
teach me how to listen to and care for my body's needs
sing me a sweet lullaby and rock me to sleep when I worry
slow me down and get me present when I'm in a hurry
help me not to fight my naps and to see the value of rest
remind me to rely on you and that your will for me is best
nurture me with your Holy Spirit and your loving word
whisper that you are with me and my cries are always heard
reveal to me how to feed my soul and find fulfillment in you
encourage me to give myself grace as I navigate the new
teach me how to walk with my head held high
inspire me to approach life with an open heart and an open mind
advise me on how to get back up when I stumble and fall
find me when I'm lost and reflect my worth when I feel small
demonstrate how to love myself and others without conditions
coach me to be my authentic self without fear or inhibitions
lead me to use discernment as I follow my curiosity
prompt me to play, create and share with generosity
train me to be patient when things don't go my way
fortify me to find my security through my faith
reassure me to trust you fully as I devote my life to you
support me in taking inspired action as my inner knowing
        guides me to
instruct me about the power of my words and beliefs
embolden me to speak truth and to act with integrity
focus me on my purpose and on pursuing my wildest dreams
cheer me on as I follow my joy and envision possibilities

nudge me to feel grateful, beholding the magic in the mundane
uplift me with silver linings and the growth that accompanies pain
call me to maintain hope and to see things through your eyes
enlighten me on how to be confident and humble at the same time
aid me to find my balance and live in harmony with nature
refine me to honor the sacred and embody the peace of my creator
prepare me to be courageous and follow the calling on my heart
guide me to relish the freedom and abundance you impart
lead me to my community of souls with whom I resonate
activate me to shine your light especially on darker days
facilitate me embracing change and forgiving and letting go
remind me that no matter where I am you are always home
help me to live in reverence and to bring you all the glory
invite me to share your wisdom and write a beautiful new story
teach me how to spread my wings and finally learn to fly
show me what it means to be the daughter of the most high[30]

Love

What does Love *look* like?

a colorful sunset
the brightest smile
mountain lake landscapes
a radiant starry sky
flower fields in bloom
a tender gaze
puppies playing
brilliant rainbows

What does Love *smell* like?

oxygen from the redwood trees
a French bakery
lavender
rain
clean laundry
scented candles

What does Love *sound* like?

a harmonious symphony
morning birds chirping
a baby's laughter
gentle purring and cooing
"no matter what you do I will always care for you"
"you can leave for as long as you need, I will always be here"
"I hear you, I see you, I understand you, I accept all of you"

What does Love *taste* like?

a soothing cup of tea
chocolate covered strawberries
farm to table
ice cream on a hot day
a perfect creamy avocado
freshly baked cookies

What does Love *feel* like?

sunshine
a heartfelt embrace
a cozy blanket
floating in warm waters
a soft breeze tickling your skin
cuddling up in front of a fireplace
safety, relief, peace, a long exhale
heaven on earth

Dancing with My Shadow

Dancing in my room in the wee hours of the night
silent disco in my ears, turned off all the lights
my astronaut projector with the nebula and stars
transports me to outer space somewhere vast and far
somehow this projected image strangely feels like home
maybe this is similar to where my soul is from
sometimes when I close my eyes I see a similar scene
a galaxy of swirling lights that makes me feel serene
as I dance I suddenly notice that I am not alone
there's a shadow on the wall having a dance party of her own
initially it startled me to see this figure moving
blocking out the light in the spots where she was grooving
logically I knew this shadow was just a part of me
mirroring my moves and always letting me lead
and yet I felt a little bit unsettled by her presence
an unexpected guest with a mysterious essence
the further I moved away from her the larger she became
towering over the ceiling and taking up more space
so I moved in closer to see what she would do
shrinking down in size, she was still copying my every move
finally warming up to her I extended out my hand
having a dance partner was not something I had planned
accepting her into my experience indeed felt necessary
to fully embrace all parts of me even those a tad bit scary
dancing with my shadow I could feel her joy as mine
with unconditional love we will be one in no time

Human BEING

I am learning how to be a human being
it's not what I do but how I do it
what is my intention
how am I showing up
am I truly present, open and connected
that's the actual goal
that's real achievement

Deepest Desires

There are desires I hold so deeply that I almost dare not desire them:

to be seen and understood and accepted for exactly who I am
to be loved so purely by another that I can melt safely into
    their arms
to live in a state of peace and joy and radiate it to the world
to feel secure enough to express the overflow of love in me
    to those around me
to let go of attachments and expectations and move forward
    in complete trust
to feel confident enough to take risks and make mistakes
    without fearing judgment
to pursue my passions with humility and without worrying
    about material success
to approach each moment in life with presence and curiosity
to fully release the impulse to plan, predict or control in
    a misguided effort to feel safe
to trust that God will always provide and meet my needs
    better than I could myself
to feel grateful for the whole range of human experiences
to have my heart mended and treated with reverence and care
to forgive myself and everyone who has hurt me
to step fully into my power, freedom, authenticity and divine
    identity
to use my voice and my gifts in service of humanity and for God's
    glory
to fulfill my mission and purpose on this earth while I am here

to share the wisdom God has revealed to me over lifetimes
to shine like the moon for others in their dark times
to accept things as they are while maintaining hope that they can
    change
to fully release people pleasing and any responsibility for others
to be fiercely protective of my inner child in all circumstances
to connect with my soul family, soul friends, and soul mates
to be part of a loving, supportive, authentic, inspiring, uplifting
    community
to feel worthy of receiving and deserving of God's blessings
to see beyond the illusions of this world with discernment and become
    more like God
to feel safe in the world without feeling like I have to look over my
    shoulder
to live in a world where love and kindness are the norm and peace
    abounds
to live with full awareness of how I am co-creating my own reality
to see the world through the eyes of a child, with awe and wonder at
    the little things
to live an expansive creative life that delights me and keeps things fresh
to learn the sweet spot of feeling my emotions and letting them move
    through me
to become the most patient and understanding version of myself
to love the skin I am in and fully appreciate and take care of my body
to live in harmony with Mother Earth and appreciate all the seasons
    of life
to make decisions that are loving towards myself and for the highest
    of all involved

to see the divinity in all living beings, even those who don't see it in
themselves

to experience adventure and fun and enjoy all the magic life has to
offer

to seek first the kingdom of God[31] and feel secure, balanced, aligned,
whole and fulfilled

to experience more than just fleeting moments of heaven on earth

to inhabit the land that flows with milk and honey[32], with the
abundance and sweetness of living in unity with God

I hold these desires so deeply that I must dare to believe them
possible, release them and feel grateful for them. Maybe I'll see them
when I believe them, aka having faith.

God's Love Language

Chatting with Jesus on Valentine's Day
I requested he be my valentine and show me the way
he is able to love me from another dimension
asking about his love language with playful intention
as the day unfolded I began to receive
the sweet little gestures he was sending for me
every detail reminded me he knows me so well
and his thoughtfulness surpasses that of anyone else
each of the love languages were well represented
in his infinite ways they were even transcended
there was something he gave me that no one else could
a feeling inside that felt so very good
uplifting my spirit throughout the whole day
with a joy and a peace that can't be taken away
I understood that while external things are often fleeting
the love of my creator is enduring and completing

Thanksgiving

There was an aching in my heart when I awoke today
and realized it's another lonely holiday
Thanksgiving dinner was always your favorite
surrounded by family and food and merriment
recalling the last one we spent together
you wrote a song about changes of seasons and weather
how painful to know that we can't go back
that we'll never experience the traditions we once had
of all of the things God removed from my life
you were the most precious to me by a mile
I head to the beach seeking comfort for my soul
taking my heavy heart out for a nature stroll
warm salty tears stream down my cheeks
cleansing my sadness, longing and grief
picking up stones like the ones we used to share
I pray you are with me in spirit and care
from behind the clouds the orange sun peaks out
shifting the mood, reminding me what this day's about
giving thanks for all that God has provided
with presence my appreciation and joy are ignited
learning to hold space for all the range of feels
keeping my mind sound as the heaviness heals
a hopeful thought enters as I envision a new life
waiting on the other side of this emotional strife
with new traditions and relationships that I have yet to meet
wonder what surprises God has curated for me
one day when I spend a holiday no longer alone
I will smile and think of you and relish it that much more

Semiconductor

Interacting with the world
entering a room
or in my imagination
the energy moves through

Alchemized, transmuted
elevated, changed
a gift by higher authority
to leave things rearranged

Sometimes it is conscious
sometimes unawares
many times it's guided
by divine state of affairs

Often times I bite off
more than I can chew
leaving me indisposed
as I purge the residue

When the energy triggers
something deep inside
those then are my shadows
from which I cannot hide

Interacting with the world
the energy moves through
leaving spaces better off
is what I love to do

True Identity

Who am I to you God?
how do you see me?
what purpose did you create me for?
what is my true identity?

My child, I created you for so many reasons
your life will be comprised of different seasons
you are here to blossom, to bloom, to grow
you will venture where many will never go
you are my beloved child with whom I am well pleased[33]
everything you do you can do with ease
you are a force of nature, a powerful source of love
when you struggle know you have support from above
you are my precious diamond, you shine so bright
you are a falcon getting ready to take flight
take my hand child, we are in this together
as birds of a feather we flock together
I am in you and you are in me[34]
that is the truth of your identity
daughter of the most high[35], you are royal by birth
you are in the world but not of this earth
you are a little taste of heaven for those you come across
as you radiate my peace from your open heart
you are a seer of truth, seeing beyond the illusions
with each layer you shed you step out of the confusion
I gave you a voice that's meant to be heard
magnifying the impact of your sacred words
you are a mirror for others who struggle to see
their own worth and divinity

I am proud of you child for stepping into your power
for embracing your true essence of a wildflower
for trusting me and giving me free reign over your life[36]
for taking the road less traveled and holding your head high
my dear, you are a bridge from the darkness to the light
paving the way for others also yearning to take flight

Dear Men

How I feared you for so long
how I blamed you for so long
how I hated you for so long
how I fled from you for so long

How I dreamed of you for so long
how I desired you for so long
how I ached for you for so long
how I pursued you for so long

How I gave you power over me for so long
how I changed myself for you for so long
how I worked for your approval for so long
how I allowed you to objectify me for so long

It wasn't you, it was me
well it was you AND me
I forgive myself, I forgive you
I am waving my white flag

All Roads

Making choices every day on this spiritual path
analysis paralysis as I fear incurring wrath
expectations that I make the most "perfect" decision
try to follow guidance but don't always have clear vision
when I veer off on a path that turns out incorrect
leading to some struggle or rejection or dead end
it may take time and energy to recalculate my route
but each wrong road I've taken has taught me something new
aware now of the truth that mistakes are to be expected
and one way or another we will always be redirected
to the places meant for us which are our destiny
as all roads lead us to the same result eventually
yes the higher road may have less bumps and a better view
but sometimes we need contrast to get us where we are headed to
whatever way I travel I have finally understood
that God will use my detours and adversities for good[37]
most importantly is not to take it all so serious
sometimes misdirection brings significant experience
best to follow joy and let my heart lead the way
I move with more alignment when there's stillness in my day
giving myself grace as I navigate the unknown
remembering that on our journeys we are not alone
making choices every day on this spiritual path
I know I needn't fear for he always has my back[38]

True Security

I used to feel secure knowing that I had a family to support me
        then one day God opened my eyes to the truth
I used to think my safety lied in being part of a community
that shared my culture
        then one day God opened my eyes to the truth
I used to believe I was okay as long as I had friends to rely on
        then one day God opened my eyes to the truth
I used to think finding a husband and "settling down"
would bring the ultimate stability
        then one day God opened my eyes to the truth
I used to believe a degree, career, steady job and income
were the keys to my security
        then one day God opened my eyes to the truth
I used to feel I was safe because I had a house to live in
and creature comforts
        then one day God opened my eyes to the truth
I used to think I was okay because I lived in a free country
with certain rights
        then one day God opened my eyes to the truth
I used to see my daily routine and adherence to a to-do list
as my source of stability
        then one day God opened my eyes to the truth

Piece by piece, he has dismantled my sense of security in anything
    other than him
my world has crumbled time and time again
every time a rug gets pulled out from under me, I am disoriented,
    I fear, I grieve
every time I get back up I am stronger, more empowered and more
    confident in myself
he has shown me the steep price I paid and trade-offs I made in my
    quest for safety
I see now the power I gave to people and circumstances outside
    of myself
I see now the ways I traded my authenticity in search of acceptance
    and belonging
I see now the ways I prioritized others' views over my own heart
I see now that I built a whole life on unstable ground

My eyes are wide open now, and the source of my true security is clear
each step of the way he has shown me that I can trust him
each step of the way he has shown me that he believes in me
each step of the way he has reassured me that he is always with me
    and for me
his love has shown me that I can face challenges, take risks, and
    surrender more fully
as I rise from the ashes I am rebuilding my life on the secure
    foundation of my faith

An Ode to Music

Behold the power of music
whispering its many truths
bypassing logic and reason
and giving us license to move

As diverse as our very humanity
with frequencies for one and all
an avenue for divine expression
that can easily bring down walls

Connecting us to our hearts
and our bodies as well
filling up auditoriums
and the places where we dwell

It often tells our stories
so we feel seen and known
lifting our very spirits
helping us feel less alone

Joining us with others
during celebratory times
creating blissful memories
throughout our lifetimes

Singing is therapeutic
dancing brings release
forgetting the weight of our worlds
with moments of presence and peace

Sometimes it's on a mission
to make the world a better place
reminding us of our oneness
enveloping us with grace

Guiding us back to our true north
inspiring us to dream
facilitating worship
and making us feel serene

The soundtrack of our lives
may change throughout the years
but one thing remains constant
music is always near and dear

What Could Go Right

What could go wrong when I step into the spotlight
to share meaningful messages for people far and wide
images of catastrophes swirling in my head
going as far as seeing me winding up dead
fears of rejection, humiliation and harm
attacks from the enemy, straight jacket around my arms
what if they're not ready or they misunderstand
what if I enrage them when I finally take my stand
what if they try and silence me with mean-spirited words
what if the mirror I show them makes them take up their swords
what if they're happy sleep walking and hate that I'm awake
what if they oust me publicly and burn me at the stake
fears of being persecuted for my spiritual gifts
afraid of standing alone unsupported through these shifts
what if they just don't care and all this is for nothing
somehow that alternative feels safer than the shunning
notice I am ruminating in pessimistic dramas
what if all these what ifs are just remnants of my trauma
maybe the problem is I have been asking the wrong question
and pushing past my fears will take loving intervention
aware of my creative powers I decide to flip the script
focusing on what could go right I'll be better equipped
to step into the calling God has placed on my life
a lighthouse to help people through their darkest nights
what if others heal and grow from the messages I share
what if being vulnerable is the only way there
if you light it he will write it, you're a vessel after all
trust that you have been prepared to answer the call

reminding me I'm not alone, he is always by my side[39]
guiding and protecting me, it's safe for me to shine
this mission has never really been about me anyway
but rather letting him lead me so I can show them the way

Library

Go towards the brightness, smell the sea
feel the fresh air and sunshine on me
all of these books with stories to tell
some are so quiet, some seem to yell
subjects are ranging from serious to light
a glimpse into others' inner worlds and plights
pulled to the kids' area by my inner child
back to simpler times, allowed to be wild
wall creatures greet me with glad exclamation
books with bright pictures and fun explanations
wish we could stay in this season of whimsy
before this harsh world left our pages so flimsy
perhaps I'll remain just a little bit longer
as my narrative heals and my life text grows stronger

Let It Shine

I was born with a veil over my eyes
without the capacity to see my own light
the people around me could see it in me
prompting them to either draw closer or flee
my empathy picked up on people's discomfort
I turned down the dimmer switch to appease all the squinters
over time my blind fold grew thicker and thicker
as messages from this world chipped away at my brilliance
making myself small and silencing my voice
masking to please others felt like the safer choice
feeling like a burden and unworthy to receive
I buried my creativity and watered down my dreams
faith took a back seat to fear-based volition
overanalyzing took precedence over following my intuition
I stumbled into the valley of the shadow of death[40]
encountering my demons and falling into the depths
unsure if I would survive these darkest of days
asking God for a lifeline, he finally removed the veil
overwhelmed by my own light, I became a squinter too
afraid of what this illumination might lead to
I flipped off the switch to try and make things feel right
confused by this roller coaster of darkness and light
my pupils just needed more time to adjust
after all I had been through it was difficult to trust
that I can truly leave behind this life I've outgrown
and embody the full power and brightness of my soul
now that I know the truth about this radiant light of mine
I'm ready to embrace it and finally let it shine

Creator

Living in reaction trying to just get through the day
helpless moving through having given power away
focused on surviving long after the threat was gone
nervous system fried from much fear of being wrong
duped by matrix programming and socio-cultural ills
running on autopilot, what a poor use of free will
having been made in the image of the one who created all[41]
he invited me to be more like him and I humbly answered the call
speaking the world into existence by uttering "let there be light"[42]
he showed the power of the tongue to bring forth death and life[43]
as I shift and step into my divine identity
buoyed and provided with spiritual authority
recognizing the power I've been entrusted with to create
aware of choice in each moment to live in brand new ways
from trying to predict, grasp and control out of fear
to letting it all go and trusting the path will be made clear
the paradox of living in empowered surrender
present and magnetic, we are doing this together
a little c creator aligning my heart and will
to the Creator of the universe who promises to fulfill
a future of inspiration and abundance so sweet
anything is possible with the creator in me

Sunflower Friend

Everyone needs a sunflower friend
a ride or die who's got your back through thick and thin
someone to turn to on the cloudy days
to remind you you are worthy and loved always
they uplift your spirit when you are feeling down
and hold up a mirror so you can see your own crown
radiating warmth and positive energy
they provide a safe space for full vulnerability
in the midst of your storms they shine a bright light
giving greater clarity as you navigate the dark night
they are powerful and confident and full of grit
their strength is contagious to those who witness it
accepting all versions of you as you grow and change
they celebrate your successes and comfort you through your pain
you can dream together without limitations
you can show up without a formal invitation
they are generous with their time and intentional with their attention
providing joy, hope and healing without demanding reciprocation
much like the sun they are adept at giving
and proximity to them helps you thrive and keep living
time flies when I am with my sunflower friend
she is a gift that keeps on giving to no end
I love when our inner children play together
when we laugh, when we cry, whatever the weather
I always thank my lucky stars for aligning our paths
what a blessing to have a friendship built to last

Speeding Ticket

Slow down child, enjoy the view
I want to show you something new
don't be afraid of uncharted paths
rushing past them as you have
heading back towards what is known
familiar pastures where you've roamed
I have no more to show you there
driven by your ego scared
seeking safety in comfort zones
yet they no longer feel like home
it's time to trust me to take the wheel
release control so I can reveal
the wonders of doing life with me
the joie de vivre of a mind set free
slow down child, enjoy the view,
as I take you somewhere completely new[44]

Rest and Realign

I woke up with a feeling of sadness in my heart
of emptiness and dread, not wanting the day to start
a freeze response triggered by the world's chaos and fear
ruminating thoughts of what I'm even doing here
frustrated to be experiencing this darkness once again
judging what is processing through, starting to complain
avoidance and distractions as I try and numb the feeling
planning and controlling, seeking exit from this reeling
looking to the future and making a list to do
cleaning, shopping, eating, scrolling, anything to get through
but whatever I put my mind to doesn't seem to work out
as I realize I seek relief not within but without
having done this countless times somewhere in me I knew
that resistance is futile and the only way out is through
taking a moment to get still, to rest and realign
tuning into my heart and connecting with the Divine
allowing in all that is demanding to be felt
witnessing with loving presence, holding space well
big release as tears flow and energy is moving
big relief as I'm made aware of the angst that has been brewing
fears around being stuck in the wilderness forever
healing from the healing process is its own endeavor
shown I'm not being punished or abandoned or held back
but rather being refined and equipped to continue on this path
seeing the higher perspective helps me get back in the flow
with patience now accepting where my guidance wants to go
in a state of presence I am able to receive
the clarity and wisdom and ability to perceive
a profound sense of gratitude that comes with feeling alive
rest and realignment are essential for us to thrive

Old Dresser

I have created a lovely home with the simple goal
of bringing in that which speaks directly to my soul
a peaceful cozy nest where I can truly rest
a sweet sanctuary where I feel my very best
out of the corner of my eye I suddenly see
an old dresser that for years has been with me
I notice it doesn't match my new clean aesthetic
yet somehow it has survived all the moves and redecorating
I wonder what this dresser is still doing in my place
mismatched with my decor, it doesn't fit the space
sitting in the entry way an energy all its own
a major feng shui no-no as its presence blocks the flow
what am I even keeping in the dresser these days?
with curiosity I open the drawers and much to my dismay
I find loads of old junk that I thought I had released
relics of a past life that no longer suit me
symbolizing old ways of thinking and being
with emotions tucked away that I wasn't feeling
addictions, distractions, old stories all cluttered
memories and secrets that I'd rather not utter
I tune in to get a sense of what the dresser means
it seems to be a block to fully allowing in God's peace
a physical manifestation of my difficulties letting go
and trusting in a future the plans for which I do not know
understanding I no longer need the contents of these drawers
as God gives me a whisper, "I am with you, peace is yours"
a tingling in my hands ignites a new reaction
the power is within me to take necessary action
it's time to say goodbye and leave the old dresser behind
and most importantly I must clear the dresser in my mind

My Love Remains

When you are having a difficult day
my love remains
when your worries and fears take over
my love remains
when you cry, when you scream
my love remains
when you numb yourself and avoid feeling
my love remains
when you go looking for fulfillment in the wrong places
my love remains
when you are disconnected from yourself and your surroundings
my love remains
when you lose something or someone important to you
my love remains
when you make a mistake or harmful decision
my love remains
when you sabotage your own progress
my love remains
when you get distracted and lose your way
my love remains
when your faith is weak and faltering
my love remains
no matter what you do or where you go
my love remains
I am always with you, waiting for you to notice and come home[45]

Waiting Season

In the waiting season feeling frustrated and stuck
confused about next steps, being held back while in flux
seems like it's been ages and yet things look the same
waiting on his blessings, what is causing this delay
where's the external reflection of the shifts I've made within
trying to push things forward as my patience wears thin
nothing is as it should be and nothing is as it seems
striving in desperation in hopes the light will soon turn green
is it time to pivot, time to go on on my own?
wondering how much longer it can persist, my weary soul
but those who wait on the Lord do renew their strength[46]
God is not in hustle culture, he is playing the long game
you cannot rush the fruits that are growing on a tree
the butterfly can't leave the chrysalis a second early
he assures me that I am right where he needs me to be
that I must trust him as he is working behind the scenes
the wait is never wasted in his glorious hands
once we let go and let God get us ready for his plans
though we might not understand exactly what he's doing
the one who sees it all and who is always moving
he'll know when the time for a change of scenery has come
in the meantime I will stay in aligned appreciation
because his timing is precise, he is never late
there is enormous power in staying faithful in the wait[47]

Divine Feminine

The awakening of the divine feminine is upon us
that sacred life-giving force residing in each and every one of us
having been silenced and oppressed by a world upside down
aching for nurturing and compassion scarcely found
as the deceptions of patriarchy are widely revealed
and the wounds of sexism we internalized are healed
though our past contributions have received little credit
and telling herstory would require major edits
how frightened the world has been of a woman's power
regulating wombs, burning witches and electing hateful cowards
but the feminine will not be held down any longer
as the truth is exposed and our voices grow stronger
we are not looking for revenge or to play the victim
we are claiming our rightful place as leaders of emerging new systems
where the lopsided prizing of the yang is transcended
and the value of the yin in all things is comprehended
a balance so exquisite between doing and being
a harmonious interplay of initiating and receiving
reconnecting to our deepest emotions and intuition
as we soften and flow and help guide the transition
from an old earth plagued with depravity and greed
to the new earth abundant with love, joy and peace
where we lift each other up and rise together
as whole complete beings we don't fixate on gender
bringing heaven to earth[48], everyone is included
as we lead the way forward we are firmly rooted
in the wellspring of wisdom provided by the Divine
it is time for the feminine to let her light shine

Seeing Beyond

I've been sitting with this ominous feeling for months
my spidey-sense going off of danger to confront
a hateful toxic rhetoric has fully taken power
sewing chaos and division in hopes that we will cower
threatening to take us back to the darkest of ages
oppressing our most vulnerable, humans locked in cages
adrenaline coursing through my body as my mind runs amok
helplessness and horror threaten paralysis and getting stuck
and yet when I tune into my soul there's a hopeful anticipation
aware that all this turmoil is providing an invitation
to see beyond the veil of this physical existence
and awaken to the truth of the quality of our systems
built on a foundation of corruption and greed
neglecting responsibility for caring for those in need
as the pendulum swings deep into the dark
we must source our light within and share our divine spark
when we evolve our consciousness and raise our frequency
the shadowiest parts of us come up to be released
to create a new world the old must first be seen
a mirror for each of us to realize where we've been
in scarcity, survival, control and deception
in victimhood, in fear and the illusion of separation
if we can see this onslaught for what it really is
the dying breath of a dragon that has already been killed
and focus our gaze towards the future we want to see
one where love is plentiful and humanity is at peace
where all people are valued and feel safe to just be
authentic, expansive, joyful and free

new systems built with inclusive intention
with compassion and hope and a faith restoration
attending to Mother Earth and holding the knowing
that we are all connected and abundance is flowing
so friends I ask you to join me in this sacred mission
as we empower ourselves to bring forth a brand new vision

The Revolution is Within

Can you feel the energy of revolution in the air
the people demanding a greater level of care
the hierarchy of power and control based in fear
profit over people, the matrix to which we adhere
a people divided so we are blinded from seeing
that we are all one and powerful beings
an us versus them, dehumanization
blaming and scapegoating, stuck in victimization
how do we go about bringing about change
is it anger and violence, do we continue to cast blame?
can we sustain a revolution outside of ourselves
if the conflict within us continues to swell
as within, so without, the saying goes
these systems are mirrors of our internal woes
reflecting our history of trauma and oppression
this survival dynamic will require transcendence
what if we take a moment to look within
to explore our inner landscape where peace has not been
to find where we have given our power away
when our minds are in shackles true freedom can't stay
let us heal the turmoil that has plagued us inside
to fight the darkness we must first find our own light
we must surrender that which we cannot control
and take responsibility for our actions and roles
grace and compassion reveal the path we dream of
to find a way forward we must first feel our own love
stepping into our truth and power, we cannot be controlled
the illusion of the enemy can no longer hold

only then can our voices truly be heard
a choir of harmonies proclaiming the word
when the flame of revolution is lit from within
our collective torch of change will at long last win[49]

Heart-Centered Living

The walls around our heart
we build up to protect
are the same walls blocking us
when we seek to connect

If we shut out the pain
we shut the joy out too
we have little to gain
and everything to lose

The safety of the armor
of leading with the mind
decisions based in logic
leave a vital part behind

The heart serves as the bridge
from our human to our spirit
connecting us with the Divine
allowing us to inherit…

The wisdom of our guidance
from a deeper knowing
reconnecting with our hearts
in no time we'll be glowing

Flying off a Cliff

When I think about moving forward something gives me pause
as tension fills my neck and shoulders, clenching in my jaw
impatient for new beginnings yet paralyzed by resistance
putting off inspired action despite my guides' gentle insistence
what am I afraid of? I tune in to get a sense
fears of being vulnerable and seen are among the most intense
after years of being set apart and being on my own
undergoing deep shifts and doing life alone
unsure of what living looks like outside of my bubble
especially as the world seems increasingly rife with trouble
feeling called to use my voice in service of others
I'd shy away from the spotlight if I had my druthers
closer to the edge of a cliff terrified I may fall
my inner child digs her heels in fearing the unknown of it all
the struggle to feel ready seems a key part of the process
building faith and resilience as I continue making progress
emergence cannot be rushed but must occur in divine timing
taking one step after another as systems are aligning
when the butterfly finally makes an exit from her chrysalis
she hangs onto it for a bit while first expanding her wings
God reminds me lovingly that I have wings as well
and venturing towards my future will feel more like flying as I excel
though at times I may stumble, he will not let me fall
he will be my safety net protecting me through it all
holding my hand as he leads me to the plans he has for me
flying off a cliff may be more exciting than it once seemed

Soul Family

My heart cries out for my soul family
the lovers, the artists, the ones soft like me
a lone puzzle piece with no pieces around
I have looked far and wide and so far haven't found
the humans with whom I can truly fit in
when can I meet them, where have they been
is my heart fully open, am I ready to trust
my fellow beings who are made of stardust
flying V in the sky with one bird on its own
I never imagined myself soaring alone
maybe I was just set apart for a season
to find myself first, perhaps that's the reason
I suppose they have important work to do
holding the light for this world full of gloom
I can't wait to meet them, they'll feel just like home
uplifting, inspiring, unique each their own
together we play, we create, we dream
we hear one another and say what we mean
we're there for the laughs and the tears as well
envisioning my soul family makes my heart swell

Unlocked- A Fairy Tale

Once upon a time there was a little girl who was scared
of drawing the attention of those entrusted with her care
she picked up on the message it was safer to play small
longing for acceptance she dimmed herself and put up walls
betraying her true nature she stopped creating and expressing
abandoning lovely parts of herself and emotionally suppressing
she locked up her authentic voice and threw away the key
disconnected from her essence, blinded to her divinity
one day as God was healing her and calling her out of fear
that locked door swung wide open and the block in her throat was
    cleared
inhabiting her full self she began to speak and write and sing
opening floodgates of emotion and insights through her expressing
with new channels opened she stepped more fully into her power
getting out of her comfort zone and into her spirit of a wildflower
what a joyful reunion with her true nature and special gifts
a crucial part of her journey and sacred purpose to uplift
as she shared her loving energy a new freedom flowed through
following her curiosity and her highest excitement too
understanding she was safe now to be genuinely seen
she could live in the present moment and her days could be serene
she learned that she was worthy and allowed to take up space
belting out song lyrics letting her voice fill the whole place
as the now fully grown woman's heart was softening and mending
the little girl inside her celebrated this very happy ending

I Just Wanna Spread Love

I just wanna spread love
it's what my heart wants to do
smile at a stranger
protect those in danger
oh I just wanna spread love

I just wanna spread love
it's just what I was made for
hug those with heartache
bake them a nice cake
cause I just wanna spread love

I just wanna spread love
it's my favorite activity
singing a sweet song
for all to dance along
well I just wanna spread love

I just wanna spread love
it's my reason for being
help people feel seen
and know they're amazing
how I just wanna spread love

I just wanna spread love
it's overflowing from me
humor with light jokes
uplift with cute notes
yes I just wanna spread love

I just wanna spread love
it's all I came here to do
can't spread it fast enough
can't spread it far enough
oh I just wanna spread love

Through God's Eyes

If only they knew how much they are loved
that they are adored and valued from above
if they could see themselves the way I see them
through the eyes of a parent who birthed perfection
they walk around guarded and worried and rushed
disengaged from each other in constant mistrust
unaware of the pleasures I place in their paths
as their minds wander into the future and past
slumped over their phones seeking crumbs of connection
while around them a world turns with little attention
trying to get through, to get by, to survive
oblivious to the greater plans I have for their lives
unable to see their own mirrored reflection
feeling unworthy of even their own care and affection
if only they looked up more perhaps they would know
that my infinite love for my children overflows

White Ladder

I have a vision of climbing a white ladder to the sky
persevering through obstacles, including my own mind
sometimes I wonder if I'm really strong enough
sometimes I get tired and think about giving up
sometimes I'm afraid of heights and worry I may fall
sometimes it gets lonely and tough to bear it all
but his hand is leading me up each step of the way
he's able to keep me going even through the hardest days
looking back I can't believe I've made it up this high
when I reach the top I get onto his back and then we fly

What a Feeling Is Believing

Walking through life with a deep-seated belief
that I am not capable of achieving my dreams
somehow I am less than, can't do what others do
fears of taking risks and of failure to name a few
after healing upon healing, one day something shifted
the block was removed, the doubt had been lifted
I looked in the mirror and saw an extraordinary being
brilliant and inspired, a revelation so freeing
that I could do anything, nothing is out of reach
that what I have been seeking is also seeking me
with a sense of possibility I see the future through new eyes
envisioning the life that my heart truly desires
an internal alarm goes off alerting me of danger
rooted in past trauma where my shine was met with anger
a gentle reminder that I'm protected and safe
and strong enough to ward off any ill will sent my way
my belief in myself has finally surpassed all the what ifs
propelling me on my path armed with newfound confidence
knowing if others can do it, I can do it too
and if I can do it, well then so can you
we rise together as we each play a part in this vital mission
of embracing our unique gifts to serve and make our contribution
what once seemed impossible now seems like a given
as divine forces collaborate to manifest my vision
how sweet it will be to see my dreams coming true
as this feeling of believing permeates everything I do

Trust Walk

I am learning to let him lead
to take me places foreign to me
choosing things I never would
trusting he knows what's for my good
blind faith walking with closed eyes
moving as I am advised
pushing past the fear of new
healing through what I go through
knowing me and my every need
he leads me at the perfect speed
aware that he can see it all
I rely on him to catch my falls
as his gentle hand holds mine
patient while my self aligns
preparing me with every step
to receive his promises kept
anywhere he wants to go
I will wholeheartedly follow[50]

New Abilities

Undergoing reactivation of dormant spiritual gifts
suddenly more attuned to subtle bodily shifts
as the healing progresses and obstructions are removed
intuitive abilities are gradually improved
tuning in to feel and discern a deeper meaning
things are often not at all as they are appearing
surrounded by synchronicities and confirming signs
seeing mental images shown by the Divine
sensing energy blocks and flow
sacred truths that I just know
think of something and it appears
dreams with messages more clear
newfound appreciation for nature
telepathy in communication
connecting with my heart and soul
hearing where they want to go
lyrical downloads in my mind
aware of shifts between timelines
matrix glitches help reveal
what is false and what is real
letting go of witch wound fears
shedding shame with every tear
opening up my third eye wide
receiving info from my guides
been turned into a magic wand
with abilities granted for serving God[51]

Wildflower

Listen to the whisper of the wildflower
sharing wisdom with anyone who will hear
growing in the most inhospitable of places
she brings hope to those living in despair
some call her a weed and see her as a nuisance
blind to her beauty and unique contributions
threatened by her fierce and untamed ways
she doesn't act the way flowers are expected to behave
when she's stepped on she seems to grow back even stronger
so bright that you have to wear shades to gaze upon her
unapologetically making anywhere her home
though she prefers open spaces and is partial to the sun
she has an important purpose to serve
supporting a whole host of life on our earth
she generously provides from her sweet nectar
energizing the life of all those around her
she reminds us that we are all one and connected
that God provides even enough for the grasses[52]
that we can grow and flourish in the broken places
and being our true wild selves brings goodness and graces

The Eyes Tell All

I see your shadow
I see your light
I see your peace
and see your fight

I see your sadness
I see your joy
I see your questions
and see your ploys

I see your innocence
I see your age
I see your betrayal
and see your rage

I see your worries
I see your calm
I see your mistrust
and your disarmed

I see your presence
I see your gone
I see your losses
and see your dawn

I see your weary
I see your strength
I see your depth
and your wavelength

The eyes tell all
they tell your story
through them I meet
your soul's full glory

Seeing My Own Magic

I finally see it, the magic in me
that je ne sais quoi that makes me unique
the way my eyes twinkle
the way my smile warms
the way my heart cares
and my love overflows
the way my mind thinks
the way that it plays
the way that it questions
and how it creates
the way I'm inspired
the way that I dream
the way I seek miracles
and my curiosity
the way I see life as one big adventure
the way I embrace the unknown as I venture
the way I can make any moment more fun
as I aim to include and connect everyone
the way that I listen with an open mind
the way that I laugh until I cry
the way that I feel the whole range of emotions
and dedicate myself with utter devotion
the way I take pleasure in the simple things
like the shape of the clouds and a butterfly's wings
the way I appreciate the gifts I receive
like a nourishing meal and the shade from a tree
the way I seek truth and justice for all
and when my heart speaks the way I answer its call
the way that I treasure authentic connection
delighting in quirks and endearing imperfections

the way I see divinity in everyone and everything
and the way I use my power and voice to uplift
my search for deeper meaning and wisdom and growth
the way I relish my freedom and walk a path all my own
the way that I move and speak and sing
alchemizing darkness and serving as a bridge
my wildflower spirit, my shine like the moon
my shepherdess calling and propensity to attune
how did I miss seeing my essence all these years?
with my eyes newly opened my magical nature is crystal clear

Conga Line

My higher self invited me to start a conga line
she showed me moves to teach the others coming along behind
she said to engage people you must already be dancing
not everyone will join, not all are ready for advancing
maybe they will learn something from just the observation
some may judge and that's more about them and their reservations
you can't plan much ahead, just be present in the flow
depending on the music you might change the way you go
it takes a bit of courage to dance alone at the start
when people see your joy they'll be encouraged to take part
the energy you bring will indeed serve as persuasion
for others to feel free to also rise to the occasion
growing as you move each newbie adds their unique flavor
synchronized together moving with a sense of favor
feeling the rare bliss of being in oneness and connection
my higher self's fun parable for inspiring transformation

Promised Land[53]

What is this Promised Land of which they speak
rumored to be flowing with milk and honey
is it a place or dimension to which one arrives
or a consciousness, vibration, or feeling inside
could it be on the other side of my fear and doubt
might ego be blocking me from finding out
is the entrance gradual with steps over time
or do you wake up one day on the promised side
how do you know when you've made it there
is it in the journey or in the where
will my arrival be greeted with celebration
will we each be welcomed with grand elation
when we finally defeat the enemy's schemes
and claim our harvest after being redeemed
having watered those seeds in the wilderness season[54]
knowing we let it all go for great reason
all we have known and all we have been
in search of green pastures, especially within[55]
following the mysterious yellow brick road
trusting it is leading where the heart wants to go
perhaps it's embodying the highest version of me
creative, empowered, authentic and free
being refined along the way[56] so we are primed to receive
the fruits of the Spirit, his joy and his peace[57]
my love runneth over[58] as I'm lit from within
tastes of heaven on earth as the kingdom comes in[59]
living in alignment, in oneness, in glory
his promises fulfilled land us in a whole new story[60]

God's Love

Tears of awe stream down my face, love is all around me
entirely held and well embraced, new levels of cozy
stars and moonlight guide the way through the opaque night
perfectly complete in his ring of shimmering light
enveloped by his tender grace welcoming me home
I can finally breathe fresh air, nevermore alone
hope eternal springing from the tree of life's provision[61]
reunited with my source in warmest communion
I am nourished, I am rooted, I am dazzled, I am whole
everything makes sense here, peace renews my soul[62]

From Black Sheep to Shepherdess

Once an outcast, the odd one out
the one who questioned and raised some doubt
who saw the world for what it was
and knew something was profoundly off
she felt so deeply the pain of those around her
internalizing it in hopes of making it better
taking on their projected parts
so they could maintain what was false
ego defenses, armor and walls
keeping up appearances, banishing the heart
programmed to please and conditioned to dim
deafened to the whispers coming from within
empty and weary her soul longed for a change
this manner of living could not be sustained
she had an inkling she was meant for more
to love, to grow freely, to revel in joy
born into a world where she didn't belong
she was tasked with writing a whole new song
as God can use all things for good[63]
her pain became her power as she transcended victimhood
a transformation process to heal and purify
taking the raw materials and infusing them with light
called to step into her divine identity
with a mission and purpose to serve humanity
to share her voice and hard-earned wisdom
to illuminate a path and tend to God's children
with a special affinity for the outcast and lost
she leads with compassion, protecting her sheep at all costs

About the Author

Jordyn was born in San Diego, California in 1983 and named Janet Ratniewski. A descendant of Eastern European refugees to Mexico fleeing religious persecution, and parents who immigrated to the US from Mexico City just prior to her birth, she was raised in Southern California in a home comprised of Jewish European and Mexican cultures. Jordyn studied Anthropology and was pre-med at UC Berkeley, and went on to attain a dual doctorate in Clinical and I/O Psychology. Prior to her transformation, Jordyn was working as a Psychologist providing therapy and leadership development services. She had been a spiritual seeker for some time, always in search of truth and fulfillment. After the pandemic and several heavy losses of loved ones she felt called to quit her job, sell her home, move closer to the ocean, cut most social ties and focus inward. She went into a period of relative isolation for three plus years to "do the work." *Metamorphosis* is her first major creative undertaking.

Endnotes

1   The phrase "grace is sufficient" is quoted from 2 Corinthians 12:9
2   The phrase "my cup runneth over" is quoted from Psalm 23:5
3   "the sea gives and the sea clears away" is inspired by Job 1:21
4   Poem references events from Genesis 3:4-5
5   The phrase "robe of righteousness" is quoted from Isaiah 61:10
6   "being a child of God means even mistakes can lead to bliss" alludes to Romans 8:28
7   "my body is a precious gift from God and a sacred temple in which his Spirit dwells" echoes 1 Corinthians 6:19
8   "I am doing a new thing in you" echoes Isaiah 43:19
9   "made perfect in your weakness" references 2 Corinthians 12:9
10 "I am your strength, song and salvation" is paraphrased from Psalm 118:14
11 "turn your burdens over to me" is inspired by Psalm 55:22
12 "and the keys will soon be yours" echoes Matthew 16:19
13 "no weapon formed against you" is paraphrased from Isaiah 54:17
14 "take refuge in his arms" echoes Deuteronomy 33:27
15 "with faith built on a rock you will always prevail" is inspired by Matthew 7:24-25 and Luke 6:48
16 Third paragraph references John 11:25 and Romans 6:4
17 "the peace a taste of the promises from God" theme appears in Philippians 4:7, John 14:27, Psalm 29:11
18 "crowning has taken on multiple meanings" alludes to themes in James 1:12
19 The line "Father forgive them for they know not what they do" is quoted from Luke 23:34
20 "I trust you will all my heart and all my soul and all my mind" is paraphrased from joining verses Proverbs 3:5 and Matthew 22:37
21 "I trust that if I keep knocking you will open eventually" is inspired by Luke 11:9 and Matthew 7:7
22 "I trust that you use my hardships and challenges for good" is inspired by Romans 8:28
23 "I trust that you give me strength when I feel exhausted and weak" echoes Philippians 4:13
24 "I trust that you are the same yesterday, today and tomorrow" is paraphrased from Hebrews 13:8
25 "I trust in your plans to prosper me and give me a future and hope" is paraphrased from Jeremiah 29:11 (NIV)

26 "I trust that you want to ease my burdens and make my path straight" is paraphrased and inspired by Proverbs 3:6 (NIV) and Isaiah 42:16

27 "I trust in you forever with my mustard seed of faith" references the mustard seed metaphor in Matthew 17:20 and Luke 17:6

28 "leading from the wilderness to the Promised Land" references events from Joshua 3-4

29 "the site where Christ was baptized with the Holy Spirit" references events from Mark 1:9-10

30 "show me what it means to be the daughter of the most high" alludes to theme appearing in 2 corinthians 6:18 and 1 John 3:1

31 "to seek first the kingdom of God" is paraphrased from Matthew 6:33

32 "to inhabit the land that flows with milk and honey" is paraphrased from Exodus 3:8

33 "you are my beloved child with whom I am well pleased" is paraphrased from Mark 1:11

34 "I am in you and you are in me" is paraphrased from John 14:20

35 "daughter of the most high" refers to theme from 2 corinthians 6:18 and 1 John 3:1

36 "for trusting me and giving me free reign over your life" is inspired by Proverbs 3:5

37 "that God will use my detours and adversities for good" is inspired by Romans 8:28

38 "I know I needn't fear for he always has my back" echoes Isaiah 41:10

39 "reminding me I'm not alone, he is always by my side" echoes Isaiah 41:10

40 The phrase "the valley of the shadow of death" is quoted from Psalm 23:4

41 "made in the image of the one who created all" is inspired by Genesis 1:27

42 The phrase "let there be light" is quoted from Genesis 1:3

43 "he showed the power of the tongue to bring forth death and life" is paraphrased from Proverbs 18:21

44 Poem expresses some similar concepts to those that appear in Isaiah 42:16

45 Poem expresses similar theme to Romans 8:38-39

46 "but those who wait on the Lord do renew their strength" is paraphrased from Isaiah 40:31

47 Poem expresses similar theme to Psalm 27:14

48 "bringing heaven to earth" is paraphrased from Matthew 6:10

49 Poem inspired by the legacy of Martin Luther King Jr.

50 Poem expresses some similar themes as Isaiah 42:16 and Proverbs 3:5

51 "with abilities granted for serving God" alludes to theme appearing in 1 Peter 4:11

52 "that God provides even enough for the grasses" is inspired by Matthew 6:30 and Luke 12:28

53 Poem references events and themes from Exodus 3:8, Numbers 14:8, Deuteronomy 26:9
54 "having watered those seeds in the wilderness season" is similar to concepts that appear in Isaiah 43:19
55 "in search of green pastures, especially within" is inspired by Psalm 23:2
56 "being refined along the way" resembles theme appearing in Isaiah 48:10
57 "the fruits of the Spirit, his joy and his peace" is paraphrased from Galatians 5:22
58 "my love runneth over" is inspired by Psalm 23:5
59 "tastes of heaven on earth as the kingdom comes in" is paraphrased from Matthew 6:10
60 "his promises fulfilled land us in a whole new story" echoes 2 Corinthians 1:20
61 "hope eternal springing from the tree of life's provision" contains theme similar to Revelation 2:7
62 Poem inspired by artwork "Live Oak" by Sally Nicholson
   Poem echoes Ephesians 3:19
63 "as God can use all things for good" is inspired by Romans 8:28